THIS BOOK BELONGS TO:

_____

PRESENTED BY:

_____

ON:

_____

GETTING TO KNOW
GOD

by John Kosmas Skinas

CONCILIAR PRESS
Ben Lomond, California

Getting to Know God

© copyright 2005 by John Kosmas Skinas

All rights reserved.

Published by   Conciliar Press
                    P.O. Box 76
                    Ben Lomond, California 95005

Printed in Canada

ISBN 1-888212-73-X

to Maki, Sofiana, and the children to come

> Because I see God in your eyes,
> Hear Him in your laughter,
> Smell Him in your hair,
> Taste Him in your joy,
> and Feel Him in your kisses.

---

in memory of
Father Anthony Kosturos

Because of you I am in the Church;
Because of you the Church is in me.

WE
SEE
GOD

We see God in the beautiful icons when we step into church.

"Let the little children come to Me, and do not stop them; for it is to such as these that the kingdom of heaven belongs."
—Matthew 19:14

We see God in the flames of the candles we light.

"I am the light of the world;
he who follows Me will not walk in darkness,
but will have the light of life."
  —John 8:12

We see God in the sky, mountains, water, and sand.

"To the Lord belongs the earth and all it holds,
the world and all who live in it."
—Psalm 24:1

We see God in the face of every person we meet.

"We all reflect like mirrors the glory of the Lord."
  —2 Corinthians 3:18

WE
HEAR
GOD

We hear God in the hymns we sing with the choir.

"Sing to the Lord and bless His name;
proclaim His triumph day by day."
—Psalm 96:2

We hear God in the stories the reader shares from the Bible.

"Let the word of Christ dwell within you in all of its richness."
—Colossians 3:16

We hear God in the wind that blows the leaves from the trees.

"If you seek Me with all your heart,
I will let you find Me."
—Jeremiah 29:13

We hear God in the voices of those who need our help.

"Blessed are those who show mercy;
mercy will be shown to them."
—Matthew 5:7

WE
SMELL
GOD

We smell God in the incense that rises toward heaven.

"Let my prayers rise like incense."
—Psalm 141:2

We smell God in the Holy Gifts Father holds up high.

"Every good and perfect gift is from above, and comes down from the Father of lights."
—James 1:17

We smell God in the sweet scent of a baby.

"To You I was committed at birth;
from my mother's womb You have been my God."
—Psalm 22:10

We smell God in the flowers that come with springtime.

"Let everything that breathes praise the Lord."
—Psalm 150:6

WE
TASTE
GOD

We taste God in the Holy Communion Father gives us.

"I am the Bread of Life.
Whoever comes to Me will never go hungry,
and whoever believes in Me will never be thirsty."
—John 6:35

We taste God in the blessed bread we share with everyone around us.

"God loves a cheerful giver."
—2 Corinthians 9:7

We taste God in the foods we enjoy eating.

"God is able to provide you
with every blessing in abundance."
—2 Corinthians 9:8

We taste God in the kind words we offer to our friends.

"A friend loves at all times."
—Proverbs 17:17

WE
FEEL
GOD

We feel God in the cross we kiss in Father's hand.

"Whoever comes to Me I will not turn away."
—John 6:37

We feel God in our hearts
when we say thank you
to Jesus and His saints.

"Give thanks to the Father who has made it possible for
you to join the saints, and with them to inherit the light."
—Colossians 1:12

We feel God in the softness of the animals He made.

"In His hand is the life of every living thing
and the breath of every human being."
—Job 12:10

We feel God in the arms of the people who love us.

"You are precious in My sight, and honored, and I love you."
—Isaiah 43:4

THERE ARE SO MANY WAYS WE CAN GET TO KNOW GOD.

A Child's Prayer

Jesus, I thank You for my eyes.
    Help me see You in everyone I meet.
Jesus, I thank You for my ears.
    Help me hear You in the voices of the poor.
Jesus, I thank You for my hands.
    Help me never use them to hurt anyone.
Jesus, I thank You for my legs.
    Help me use them to run to You.
Jesus, I thank You for my mind.
    Help me think only of good things.
Jesus, I thank You for my heart.
    Please fill it with Your love.

Another Child's Prayer

Jesus, when I'm happy,
 Help me remember Your name.
Jesus, when I'm scared,
 Help me remember Your name.
Jesus, when I'm angry,
 Help me remember Your name.
Jesus, when I'm hurting,
 Help me remember Your name.
Jesus, every minute of every day,
 Help me remember Your name.

About the Author

John Kosmas Skinas, a fiction writer whose work has appeared in various literary magazines, lives in San Francisco with his wife and children. They attend Holy Trinity Greek Orthodox Church, where John is the director of the George and Tula Christopher Recreation Center.

Acknowledgements: I owe a debt of thanks to the following people for their valuable help with this book: Anne Melson, Nick Skinas, Katrina Misthos, Demi Stone, and my amazing, ever-supportive wife, Suzanne Skinas. I also need to express my gratitude to all of the priests and churches that graciously allowed me to invade their sacred spaces with my troublesome camera. Of course, I must thank all of my little (and not so little) "models"— without you there would be no book. Finally, thank you to my parents, Kosmas and Voula Skinas, not only for planting the garden that inspired this book, but also for planting the seeds of faith in my soul.

Photo credits: All photos were taken by John Skinas unless otherwise noted.
Cover (and page 7) — My son, Maki, in the narthex of Holy Trinity Greek Orthodox Church in San Francisco.
Page 6— My niece, Clairemarie, in the chapel of the Serbian cemetery in Colma, California.
Page 8— My nephew, Jack, on vacation in Kauai, Hawaii. *Photo by Nick Skinas.*
Page 9— Students at Holy Trinity's parochial school, showing us a variety of smiles.
Page 12— Students of Holy Trinity Sunday school. In the background is a unique mosaic of a young Christ learning the carpenter's trade.
Page 13— Father Nicholas standing by paternally as a young altar boy reads the epistle at St. Nicholas Church in San Francisco.
Page 14— My nephew, Jack, in the beautiful garden near his home. *Photo by Nick Skinas.*
Page 15— Maria and Mary-Jepsy, in front of the Holy Trinity Recreation Center, where they take ballet lessons.
Page 18— Father Anthony of blessed memory. This picture is very special because Father discouraged having photos taken in church. He made an exception for this book, which benefited from his blessing and encouragement.
Page 19— The Great Entrance at St. Nicholas Church in San Francisco.
Page 20— My daughter, Sofiana, surrounded by the love of her mother.
Page 21— My niece, Clairemarie, stopping to smell the flowers.
Page 24— Father Anthony pretending to give Holy Communion. Father did not want pictures taken during the actual service because he felt that the sacrament is so sacred that photographs should not be permitted while it's being administered.
Page 25— Matusala and Robeil at the Annunciation Cathedral in San Francisco.
Page 26— My son, Maki, who loves Japanese food!
Page 27— Therese and Catherine, two more little ballerinas at the recreation center.
Page 30— Father Peter offering the cross to Clairemarie at the Holy Virgin Cathedral in San Francisco.
Page 31— My wife, Suzanne, helping Maki venerate the icon of St. Nicholas at St. Nicholas Church in San Francisco.
Page 32— My niece, Catherine, petting Lady Audra Barkley.
Page 33— My nephew, David, finding comfort in his father's arms.